I'm good at

Music

Eileen Day

Raintree

www.raintreepublishers.co.uk
Visit our website to find out more information about **Raintree** books.

To order:
☎ Phone 44 (0) 1865 888112
🖹 Send a fax to 44 (0) 1865 314091
💻 Visit the Heinemann Bookshop at **www.raintreepublishers.co.uk** to browse our catalogue and order online.

First published in Great Britain by Raintree, Halley Court, Jordan Hill, Oxford OX2 8EJ, part of Harcourt Education.
Raintree is a registered trademark of Harcourt Education Ltd.

Editorial: Nick Hunter and Diyan Leake
Design: Michelle Lisseter
Picture Research: Alan Gottlieb and Amor Montes de Oca
Production: Lorraine Hicks

Originated by Dot Gradations
Printed and bound in China by South China Printing Company

ISBN 1 844 21504 0
07 06 05 04 03
10 9 8 7 6 5 4 3 2 1

British Library Cataloguing in Publication Data
Day, Eileen
Music. – (I'm good at)
780
A full catalogue record for this book is available from the British Library.

Acknowledgements
The publishers would like to thank the following for permission to reproduce photographs: Corbis/LWA-Dann Tardif, **20**; Corbis, **21**; Gareth Boden, **12**; Heinemann Library/Robert Lifson, **7**, **8**, **9**, **10**, **11**, **14**, **15**, **16**, **17**, **18**, **19**, **22**, **23** (bongos, kazoo, drumsticks, shaker) **24**; ImageState/Russell Willison, **21**; PhotoEdit/David Young-Wolff, **5**, **23** (musician); PhotoEdit/Tom McCarthy, **6**; Photo Researchers, Inc/Ellen B. Senisi, **4**; Tudor photography, **13**.

Cover photograph reproduced with permission of Topham Picturepoint.

Every effort has been made to contact copyright holders of any material reproduced in this book. Any omissions will be rectified in subsequent printings if notice is given to the publishers.

Some words are shown in bold, **like this**.
They are explained in the glossary on page 23.

Contents

What is music?

Music is creating sounds.

When you sing or play an instrument, you make music.

You can play an instrument.

You can be a **musician**.

How do I play the drum?

A drum makes a booming sound.

You can hit it with a **drumstick**.

Bongos are a kind of drum.

You can play the bongo drums with your hands.

How do I play the triangle?

A triangle is a metal instrument.

It makes a ringing sound.

You hold the string.

You hit the triangle to make the sound.

How do I play the rhythm sticks?

Rhythm sticks are pieces of smooth wood.

They make a tapping sound.

You can keep the beat with rhythm sticks.

They make music when you tap them.

How do I play the tambourine?

A tambourine is made of wood or plastic.

It has metal bits that jangle when you shake or hit it.

You can shake a tambourine.

You can hit it with your hand, like a drum.

How do I play the kazoo?

A **kazoo** is a plastic pipe.

You hum into it to make music.

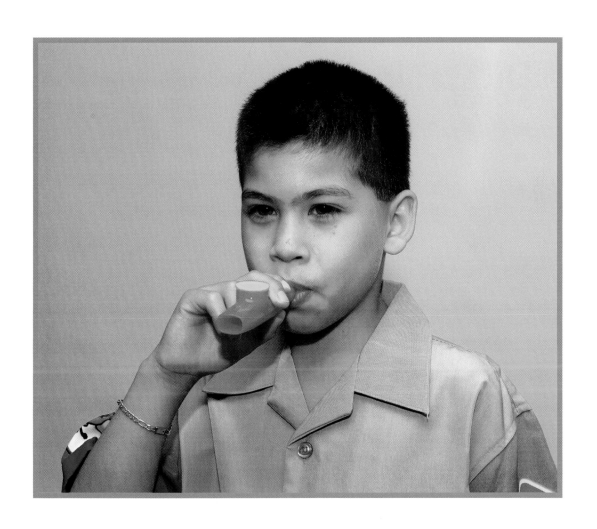

The kazoo makes your lips
feel funny.

How do I play the xylophone?

The xylophone has bars made of metal or wood.

It sounds like bells ringing.

bars

You use a beater to hit the bars.

You can play a song.

How do I play shakers?

Shakers make a rattling sound.

Seeds and shells make the noise.

There are many different kinds of shakers.

You can move the shakers to a beat.

How do I feel when I make music?

Making music makes you happy.

It is fun to create new sounds.

When you make music, you feel proud.

It is nice when people listen to you play music.

Quiz

What do you use to play these instruments?

Look for the answers on page 24.

Glossary

bongos
two small drums which are joined together

drumsticks
long, thin wooden sticks used to hit a drum

kazoo
plastic instrument you hum into to make a noise

musician
someone who makes music using instruments

shaker
instrument or anything you can make a sound out of by shaking

Index

Answers to quiz on page 22

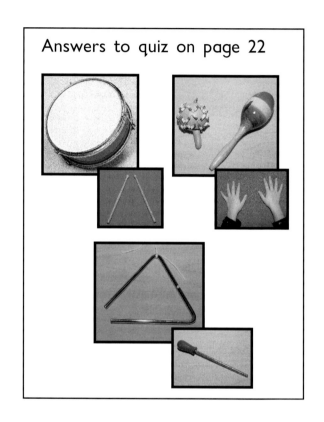

Titles in the I'm Good At series include:

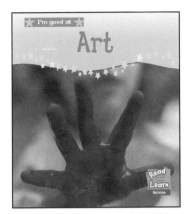

Hardback   1 844 21503 2

Hardback   1 844 21500 8

Hardback   1 844 21501 6

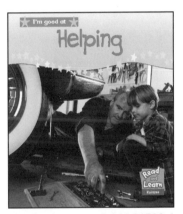

Hardback   1 844 21502 4

Hardback   1 844 21505 9

Hardback   1 844 21504 0

Find out about the other titles in this series on our website www.raintreepublishers.co.uk